WHAT IT MEANS TO BE
SERIES

PUBLISHER	Joseph R. DeVarennes
PUBLICATION DIRECTOR	Kenneth H. Pearson
ADVISORS	Roger Aubin
	Robert Furlonger
EDITORIAL MANAGER	Jocelyn Smyth
EDITORS	Ann Martin
	Shelley McGuinness
	Robin Rivers
	Mayta Tannenbaum
ARTISTS	Summer Morse
	Barbara Pileggi
	Steve Pileggi
	Mike Stearns
PRODUCTION MANAGER	Ernest Homewood
PRODUCTION ASSISTANTS	Catherine Gordon
	Kathy Kishimoto
PUBLICATION ADMINISTRATOR	Anna Good

Canadian Cataloguing in Publication Data

Elliot, Jacqueline
  What it means to be—trustworthy

(What it means to be; 21)
ISBN 0-7172-2243-8

1. Reliability — Juvenile literature.   2. Honesty — Juvenile literature.
I. Pileggi, Steve.   II. Title.   III. Title: Trustworthy.   IV. Series.

BJ1533.158E44   1987   j179'.9   C87-095064-9

Printed and bound in U.S.A

WHAT IT MEANS TO BE . . .

TRUSTWORTHY

Written by

Jacqueline Elliot

Illustrated by

Steve Pileggi

Trustworthy people can be counted on to do what they say they'll do.

Tammy was playing hopscotch with Hannah when her mother called out, "Dinner will be ready soon, Tammy. I'll be too busy to call you again, so please come inside in ten minutes."

"Okay, Mom," said Tammy.

Hannah took her turn. Then Tammy had another turn. "I'd better go in now," Tammy said when she finished. "Dinner must be ready."

"But we aren't through playing yet," Hannah pointed out.

"Yes, but I told my mother I would come in and I don't want to be late," explained Tammy. "We can play again after supper."

"Okay," said Hannah. "After supper it's my turn."

Remember to follow through on what you say you'll do so others will know that you are trustworthy.

4

Being trustworthy means always telling the truth.

Janice was playing with her dollhouse. She noticed the paint was beginning to peel. Her father had promised to give it a fresh coat of paint on the roof and in some of the bedrooms. She went downstairs to find him, but he was busy talking to a neighbor in the garden.

Instead of waiting, Janice went to the basement and found the spray gun on her father's workbench. She wondered if she could manage to paint her dollhouse herself. Just to test it, she picked up the spray gun and pulled the trigger. Paint squirted all over the bench and her father's tools. Frightened at what she had done, Janice ran back to her room.

The next day Janice's father went down to his workbench to finish building a birdhouse. He discovered that his tools were splattered with paint. He was very cross. "Who could have done that?" he wondered.

Janice was in the living room playing when she heard him ask her mother who had been using the tools. A few minutes later he came to Janice.

"Were you fooling around with my spray gun?"

"No, I wasn't," she replied.

"Well," he said to her mother, "it must have been Jason then. I'll ask him when he comes in."

When Jason got home after his baseball practice, his father asked about the spray gun.

Jason said, "No, I haven't even been in your workroom for ages, Dad."

The children's parents looked at each other. "Somebody isn't telling the truth."

Janice couldn't stand it any longer. "I did it! I didn't mean to. I only wanted to test it. You promised you would paint my dollhouse, but when I went to talk to you, Dad, you were busy." She was in tears.

Her mother put an arm around her and said, "Janice, accidents happen. Please don't be afraid to tell us when they do, even if we sometimes get angry."

"That's right," agreed her father. "We're much more concerned that you tell us the truth."

Telling the truth is the best thing to do, even if you are worried about the consequences.

Trustworthy people always look after things they borrow.

Mitchell had been busy all morning, helping his mother carry plants home from the gardening store in his wagon. She was going to fill three window boxes. Just as he was sitting down to rest on the front porch Ryan came over.

"Do you want to come to the store?" Ryan asked. "I've got some pop bottles to take back. I can't carry them by myself. We could put them in your wagon."

"I'm too tired to go with you," Mitchell said. "I've been helping my mother all morning. But you can take my wagon. Just bring it back when you're finished."

"Thanks a lot," replied Ryan. He waved to Mitchell as he pulled the purple wagon along the sidewalk.

Mitchell sat on his front porch playing with his small cars. After a while he began to worry about his wagon.

"What if Ryan doesn't come back? What if he left my wagon outside the store and someone took it?" He started to imagine all kinds of terrible things. "This is silly," he thought finally. He knew Ryan could be trusted to bring back his wagon safely.

Just then Ryan came down the street pulling Mitchell's wagon. He handed Mitchell two big black jawbreakers. "Here, these are for you," he said. "I bought them with some of the money I got from the bottles."

"Thanks, Ryan."

"Your wagon really helped me out," added Ryan.

If you are trustworthy, people know you will take care of anything they lend you.

Being trustworthy means taking special care of money that isn't yours.

Ms. Barclay held up the books of tickets so that everyone in the grade one class could see them. "Now I'm going to hand out one booklet to each of you. The tickets are fifty cents and all the proceeds will go toward buying new equipment. Does anyone have any questions?"

"If we sell all of our tickets, can we get more?" asked Dylan.

"You sure can," replied Ms. Barclay. "Hand in the money for the first ones and I'll be glad to give you another book."

"How long do we have to sell them?" asked Eva.

"Two weeks," answered their teacher.

Paul, Dylan and Ryan walked home together after school. Each of them had managed to sell two tickets.

"Just a minute," said Paul when they got to the corner store. He ran in and came back. "Here, take one," he said, handing out a licorice stick to each of his friends.

"Where did you get the money to buy these?" asked Dylan.

"From the tickets," answered Paul. "It's okay. I'll put it back when I get my allowance on Saturday."

Dylan did not approve. "That money isn't yours," he pointed out. "It belongs to the school. You're not supposed to spend any of it."

"But I'll put it back!" cried Paul.

When Paul got home he hung up his coat and went upstairs to get changed. When he came back down, he took his bag of candy into the kitchen.

"Hi," his father said. "Do you want a snack? Dinner will be late tonight since your mother had to stay late at the office." Then he noticed the bag. "Where did you get the money for candy? I thought you spent all your allowance."

Paul looked embarrassed. "I sold a couple of the tickets from school."

"And you spent the money you got for them on candy?" his father asked.

"I was going to replace it out of my next allowance," Paul mumbled.

"I'm sure you were. Still, it wasn't your money to spend, was it?"

"I guess not. I won't do it again," Paul promised.

When you're looking after money that doesn't belong to you, it's especially important to be trustworthy.

Trustworthy people can be relied upon to do their best.

Mitchell and Hannah loved jumping on the small trampolines. They always spent as much time as possible playing on them during gym class.

Miss Foster came up to them one day and said, "I've noticed how careful the two of you are on the trampolines. Would you like to be monitors?"

"Sure!" Hannah replied.

"What do we do?" asked Mitchell.

"You stand around the trampolines and make sure no one jumps too high. If someone looks like they might fall off, you put up your arms to steady them," she explained. "The grade six monitors will also be there to help you."

"That sounds fun."

Hannah and Mitchell spent the next gym class monitoring the trampolines as well as doing regular activities. By the class after that Hannah was getting bored. She found it hard to pay attention. Mitchell had to keep reminding her to look the right way and to stay alert.

Finally two of the older monitors noticed and came to talk to Hannah.

One said, "I think you've done this long enough."

"Maybe when you're older you can try again," the other added.

Hannah was very disappointed but she knew they were right.

It takes time and practice to be responsible for certain tasks. When you are placed in a position of trust, always try your hardest.

Trustworthy people can be relied upon to look after pets.

Tammy was going away for the weekend. She needed someone to look after her hamster Fergie. Hannah was too rough and noisy, and Mitchell didn't like Fergie. She decided to ask Janice.

Janice was delighted to look after Tammy's pet. Tammy showed her friend how to take care of Fergie. Janice was gentle and careful with him.

"And how much exercise does he need?" Janice asked.

"Oh, he gets lots of exercise on his wheel," answered Tammy. "But if you watch him carefully, you can let him out in your room to run around."

"And what if he gets lonely for you?"

"He likes you a lot, I can tell," said Tammy. "So just talk to him and pet him."

Tammy never worried once about Fergie all weekend. She was sure Janice would take good care of him. And she was right.

If you are trustworthy, your friends will know you can be counted on to look after their animals.

26

Trustworthy people never spread rumors.

Dylan wasn't a very good speller. In fact he almost always got the worst mark in the grade one class spelling tests. But he had decided he wanted to do well and had started studying a little bit every night. A week went by and he was ready for the spelling test.

"I'm proud of you," said Ms. Barclay as she handed back his test. "You have really improved. You got the second highest grade."

Dylan smiled. His hard work was paying off.

At recess his friends congratulated him. Some of them even asked if he would help them study.

But at lunchtime he noticed a few people staring at him and whispering. He felt uncomfortable. By the time school got out it seemed that everyone was staring at him. And no one wanted to walk home with him.

The next day Dylan saw Eva on the way to school.

"Hi," he said as he caught up to her.

She looked a little embarrassed. "Oh hi, Dylan."

"Is anything wrong?" he asked.

"Well, I heard something about you," she mumbled. "I know I shouldn't listen to stories but, uh, did you cheat on the spelling test?"

"No. I've never cheated and I never will."

"I'm sorry," Eva said. "I should have known better than to believe the story."

"Who told you I cheated?" asked Dylan, starting to feel cross.

"I don't know. Everyone seemed to be talking about it."

Dylan spoke to all of his friends and told them he didn't cheat. He asked them who had started the rumor. They all felt badly, but they didn't know who had first told them.

Dylan walked home after school feeling tired and upset. Later that afternoon Joey appeared at his door. "It was my fault," he admitted. "I started the rumor about you. You were the only one in the class who did worse than me in spelling. I was mad when you did well."

Dylan said nothing.

Joey hung his head. "I didn't know the story would spread like that," he muttered. "Really, I didn't mean to lie and have everyone think you had cheated." Still Dylan didn't answer.

"I'm really sorry," Joey said pleadingly. "I promise I'll never do it again."

"Okay," Dylan replied.

"Will you help me study for the next test?" asked Joey.

"Sure," said Dylan, "as long as you promise not to cheat or even talk about it."

"It's a deal," smiled Joey.

Making up stories about someone is a mean thing to do. If you try to imagine how you would feel if somebody told a lie about you, you'll never start a rumor about anyone else.

Friends aren't always trustworthy.

Bobby called Joey to ask if he wanted to go to the library. "I can't," Joey said. "I've got a cold and I have to stay in today."

"Oh, that's too bad," replied Bobby. "Do you want me to take your books back for you? My dad's driving me to the library, so I can pick them up."

"Sure. Thanks a lot," said Joey.

Joey gathered up his books. Then he sat by the door and waited for Bobby. He waited and waited, but Bobby didn't come.

"That Bobby," Joey said to himself. "He's forgotten all about me and now I'll have to pay a fine."

The next day Joey was still at home with his cold. The phone rang and his mother said, "It's Bobby." Joey picked up the phone.

"Hi, Joey. Are you feeling better?" Bobby asked.

"I am," Joey said, "but I'm mad at you. You said you'd take my books back, and you never came to get them."

"I'm sorry. My dad got a phone call so we didn't leave right away. Then I forgot. If you want me to, I'll come over right now and take them back."

"Well, okay," Joey answered. "If you'll really do it this time."

"I promise," said Bobby.

Even if friends haven't been completely trustworthy, you should always give them a second chance.

**It's important to develop a reputation for being
trustworthy.**

Kim and Colette were racing across the
schoolyard—they were almost late for school. They
were in such a hurry that Kim didn't notice when
she dropped her unsold fund-raising tickets.

Ms. Barclay asked everyone to turn in their
money and tickets. When it was Kim's turn, she
carefully took her money out of her bag. But the
envelope with the three unsold tickets was missing.
"Oh, no," she cried. "I can't find my tickets."

"Did you have them this morning when you left
home?" asked Ms. Barclay kindly.

"Yes," said Kim, almost in tears.

"I'm sure you didn't mean to lose the tickets,"
her teacher reassured her. "Accidents happen.
There's no need to worry about it."

The very next day, the principal called Kim down to his office. She was afraid that he was going to be angry with her for losing her tickets. He'd scold her for being careless. Worse yet, what if he thought she was lying—that she had really sold the tickets and spent the money?

"Kim," said the principal, "Ms. Barclay told me you lost three tickets."

"Yes," replied Kim.

"Well, today a young woman turned these in to my office," he said, holding up three tickets. "She said she found them in the schoolyard. I think they must be yours."

"Oh," exclaimed Kim. "That's terrific."

"Well," said the principal smiling, "you've always been truthful and responsible. We never doubted you for a moment."

If you have always shown people that you are honest and careful, they will trust you and believe what you say.

Trustworthy people can accomplish many things.

The last day of the fund-raising drive all the students gathered in the gym for a celebration. They had brought sandwiches, cookies and other treats they had made at home. There were games and balloons. Everyone had a terrific time. They had been working hard for this day so it was fun just to relax.

At the end of the day the principal announced how much money had been raised. There was enough to buy new library books, some gym equipment and a slide projector.

Trustworthy people are responsible and honest. They can be counted on to do their best. If you are trustworthy, you keep your promises. Here are some other ways you can be trustworthy:
- Always tell the truth.
- Look after things you borrow.
- Never spread rumors.
- Take special care of money that isn't yours.